How to Kindle Fire

(How to Start a Fire)

By David Aman

Photographs by Victoria Aman

This is the most basic, easy to understand book of how to make a fire that you will ever read. The many photographs and simple instructions will teach you this skill as if you were 7 years old.

This book is being written for all of those people that have trouble starting fires. Whether it is at a campfire or in a fireplace, these methods will guide you step by step to having the ability to start a fire every time. It is designed as a picture book. Rather than teach you with just words, you will actually see the steps necessary to build a successful fire.

Included in this book are lists of good tinder and how to find fuel, a trouble shooting guide and suggestions to make starting a fire easy every time. You will learn everything from how to light different kinds of matches properly to seeing pictures of different tinders that are easy to light to get your fire started.

If you have had trouble starting fires in the past, want to learn how to teach kids this skill easily or are just looking for some pointers on fire making then this is the book for you.

The basics.

Fuel + air + heat = fire.

Heat rises. That is why the flames go upwards.

The heat from the match starts the fire and then the fire creates its own heat.

IMPORTANT!

Know how you are going to put your fire out before lighting a match.

You need to have the new fuel ABOVE where the flames are.

You need to make it easy for the air to get to the BASE of the flames.

More fire.

More fuel.   More air.

Fire (heat).

Fuel + air + heat (the match).

Choosing the wood for your fire:

Look for DEAD wood to start your fire with.

Any wood that is even partially green is a poor choice.

It should be very dry. Don't choose wood that is lying directly on the ground; these will have absorbed moisture from the ground. Dead branches that are leaning against something will probably be dry because sunlight and the flow of air dried it off.

If the branch doesn't snap cleanly then it isn't dry enough. If you snap the stick and it is still partially attached then it is too green to start your fire with. The snap should sound like the sounds that come from a campfire.

If you find a stick that looks white, doesn't have any bark left on it and is not sitting directly on the ground then you have found a very dry piece of wood.

If you find one large dead branch you should have all of the different sizes of wood needed to start a fire.

You will find little thin pieces of wood at the very tips of the branch.

You will find all of the sizes of wood needed up to the larger fuel.

You do not need giant logs for your fire unless you are sitting around it telling long ghost stories.

There are 5 piles in this picture. The tinder is in the upper right, the kindling is next to the box of matches and the piles are sorted by sizes.

You should have two big handfuls of both the tinder and kindling before trying to start your fire.

Kindling is the thickness of a match stick. The pile next to the kindling is the thickness of a pencil. The next pile is the thickness of my thumb. The last pile is the fuel that will be used once the fire is going well. This fuel will keep the fire going for hours.

I kneel on my jacket to prepare the fire. The piece of paper with the arrows on it shows the direction that the wind is coming from.

Here are some types of tinder that could be brought from home.

From the upper left to the lower right they are; an old rag, a wad of duct tape, a pile of cotton balls (they don't work as great as you would think), crayons or an old candle, a wad of newspaper, a cut up soda bottle, a wad of old twine, a wad of paper cups, a piece of rubber inner tube from a bicycle, hand sanitizer that would be squirted onto a pile of kindling, fine steel wool (yes it burns), oakum (used for plumbing), cotton dryer lint.

You can find all sorts of tinder in nature.

You are looking for something that is fluffy and very dry.

Keep an eye out for this when you are hiking.

This is the down of a thistle.

These are the tops of fluffy weeds.

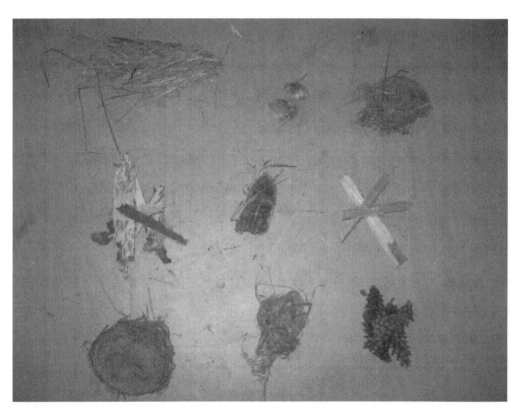

Here is some tinder I found. From the upper left to the lower right these are; dry weeds, an old bees nest and some thistle down, dry grass, white birch bark that has to be shredded, burdocks, some "fuzz sticks" that I made, a birds nest, shredded cedar bark, pine cones.

A fuzz stick is made by whittling the edges of a stick into many curls that you leave on the stick.

I used the bark from a wild grape vine to start my fire.

I took a couple of handfuls off of the vine.

I hold the bark between my hands and start moving my hands around just like peddling a bicycle.
I let the fine dust fall where the fire is going to be.

After I shredded the bark so that it was fine, I tied the long strands into a loose overhand knot.

This makes a nice, fluffy pile of tinder that will catch a flame easily.

Notice that there are about two handfuls of tinder here.

It is important to have enough tinder burning to get your kindling burning.

Your pile of tinder should be in the center and underneath the other sticks.

This is the "A frame fire lay".

I tell my Boy Scouts that starting a fire with this design is "Girl Scout easy".

Use some of your fuel sticks as the base.

Here is where the air will get under the fire.

Put your kindling loosely over your tinder.

Put your pencil sized kindling over the match stick sized kindling.

You can place some smaller pieces of fuel on top of the pile.

Notice that all sticks are piled loosely, allowing air to flow in and around everything.

Poke a hole deeply into the bottom of the pile of tinder.

This is where you will be holding your lit match when you go to light your fire.

The "Turkey lay" fire design.

This design is good to use if one of the logs that you have to use is big or if you are using burned logs left over from a fire from the previous day.

Logs that are charred because they were previously in a fire start on fire VERY easily.

Do you see that we are making a spot for the air to flow under our fire?

Loosely place the sticks that are as thick as a match over the tinder.

Loosely place some of the pencil thick sticks on top of the match thick sticks.

Don't place too many on here or else you may restrict air flow when the fire is burning.

Poke your finger deeply into the bottom of the pile of tinder.

This is where you will be holding your lit match to get the fire started.

This is the "log cabin" design with many layers on the very top.

This is a good fire design for lighting a fire in the rain.

The top layers keep the rain off of the fire until it is going very well.

A fire that is burning very well will stay lit in everything except a very heavy rainstorm.

The two little sticks in the very front allow you to leave the first horizontal stick out of the pile.

This gives you more room to light the fire.

Put pencil sized sticks onto your inner pile and then continue the log cabin style with the fuel until it is higher than your inner pile. Each layer of sticks is perpendicular to the layer below it. Each layer is made out of just two sticks until you get to the very top.

Make a couple layers of solid wood at the very top. Have the top layer perpendicular to the layer just below it. This forms a sort of roof that will keep the rain from the fire that is below.

Poke your finger deeply into the base of the tinder.

This is where you will place your lit match.

How to light a match.

This should be practiced often until you feel comfortable lighting a match.

Having children learn the proper, safe ways of lighting a match is important.

You should not be afraid of them learning this. Isn't it something we all have to learn anyways?

Isn't it better that they learn the proper handling of matches and how to be safe with them rather than learning this on their own?

Paper matches are very inexpensive but harder to light than wooden matches.

They should never be allowed to get wet or else they will be useless.

The "pinching method".

This is the easiest way to light a paper match and people feel
more comfortable lighting it this way.

Place the match over the striker strip.

Pinch the match head GENTLY between the cover and the striking strip.

Pull straight out.

If the match doesn't light then try doing it over again while pinching just a little bit harder.

The "cupped hand" method.

This is important to know in order to light a match when the wind keeps blowing the match out.

Hold the match firmly as shown.

Push down with your thumb,

Holding the match head against the striker strip.

Pull your hand away from the striker strip while moving your thumb away from the flame when it lights.

The "standard lighting method".

This is the method you will use for the rest of your life once you have learned it.

Make sure to have the match box or match book closed when lighting your match. This prevents the whole pile of matches from accidentally lighting.

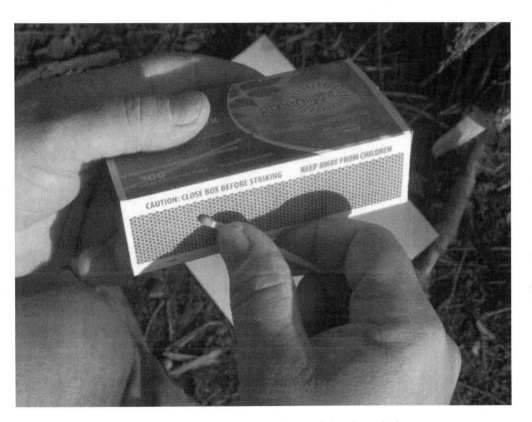

Make sure to have control of the match and have a tight grip on the box.

Slide the match sideways while holding the match head against the striker strip.

Pull your thumb down to your finger tip once the match is lit.

Don't be afraid of burning your finger. It is very easy to move your finger away before the flame burns you.

Hold the match so the flame is going upwards away from your fingers.

Make sure to have a good grip on the match.

This is done the same way as using the wooden match standard method.

The only difference is that the paper match is shorter and more flexible.

Once the match is lit you won't have much time to light whatever you are going to light.

Have some very thin kindling handy. If you light this with your paper match, you will have what is basically a longer match with which you can light your fire.

This gives you more time to get the fire lit.

Make sure to get the flame from your match UNDER the tinder and in as deep as you can get it into the pile.

Be careful not to hit the tip of your match against something. This will put your match out.

Hold the flame under the tinder as long as you can in order to make sure that the tinder is lit well.

Leave everything alone for a minute or so to allow it to get going well.

When the fire is going well, FEED THE FIRE!

I can't tell you how often people just stand back and watch the fire that they have started and don't put new fuel on it fast enough.

Remember that you want the flames that you have already to be catching new wood on fire.

This is where all of the preparation that you did before lighting your match comes in.

All of the wood that you need for the fire is sitting right there, Handy to be placed on the fire.

Put the new, larger wood over where the flames are.

You don't ever want to leave your fire unattended.

If you did not have all of your wood gathered ahead of time you would have to run into the forest looking for wood.

You will need the wood anyways, why not get it before you light your fire?

Place the sticks on the fire in a criss-cross pattern to allow for the air to flow easily.

It was the initial design that allows air to get under the fire.

Keep the spaces at the base open to allow air to flow under the flames.

AHH

SUCCESS!

How to solve problems.

1. If you can't find dry wood look on the inside of the bottom of evergreen trees. You will also find dry wood in open, sunlit areas of a dense forest. Look for branches that have fallen from a tree and are leaning up against something.
2. You light the tinder and it just smolders and keeps going out. Take you tinder out and fluff it up. It cannot be a tightly packed ball. It has to be fluffy and allow air to flow through it and that is why a pile of cotton balls doesn't work great.
3. If your fire was going well and then it kind of just started dying then it wasn't getting enough fuel or air. Either you have to spread the sticks out allowing more air to get to the inside of the fire or the fuel wasn't there to catch the flames from below. Don't be afraid to spread the sticks out more. Don't smother your fire by putting on too many sticks in a tight group.
4. Don't throw a pile of leaves on top of your fire to get it going better. This will just smother the fire and often the leaves have a lot of moisture in them that will try to put the fire out.
5. If your fire was going well and then used up the fuel above the flames then you would have to push the other sticks that are in the fire above where the flames are. I have seen fires that people allowed the center to burn up, leaving just a ring of sticks. Fuel that is on fire needs to be near other fuel that is on fire. One stick that is on fire won't stay lit for very long without another stick near it. The heat has to be contained and bounce back and forth from one hot log to the other.

Suggestions..

1. The first thing you should do before lighting a fire is to know how you are going to put it out!
2. I can't stress enough how important it is to gather a large quantity of everything your fire will need BEFORE you light a match. Preparation is a giant key to success in fire starting.
3. Clear your site that your fire will be lit in. There should be a clear 10' diameter area around where your fire is.
4. If you are using anything other than a match to light your fire then light some small twigs or a wad of tinder and use this to stick under your tinder to start your fire. It would be very difficult to light your fire with a lighter or a glowing ember unless you do this.
5. Make sure that the air can get into the base of the fire. Your initial fire design should allow for this airflow.
6. Start your fire from the CENTER of the BOTTOM of the pile. I can't tell you how often people light a match and try to start the fire from the top. Flames go upwards and start the wood that is above them on fire.
7. You have to let the fire build upwards moving from the smallest sticks upwards to larger ones and finally to the biggest fuel. YOU CANNOT LIGHT A LOG WITH A MATCH!

1. Go help out your local scout troop

Everybody knows something! They know how to fish or how to sew. They are good at pounding nails or making pie. All across the world there are organizations such as Girl Scouts, Boy Scouts, Cub Scouts, Sea scouts, Venture crews, and 4H groups that kids belong to. These children need to learn more than can be taught in school. They need to be shown skills by those who know them best. I am asking all adults to seek out these groups and see what you can do to help them, even if it is for only an hour each year. Help out these dedicated leaders teach our children. Some skills are not being passed onto our kids. A generation from now will anyone know how to make a pie crust. Will a kid be able to start a fire without the use of a match or cut a log with an axe?

You will be surprised at how much fun it can be to pass on things that you know. Even if you don't have a special skill, the help will be appreciated. These volunteers aren't doing this work for themselves. They are helping the kids grow up to be better people, more diversified and well rounded citizens. Please do anything that you can to help make our future generation the type of people that you want them to be when they rule the world.

I would like to dedicate this book

To the most wonderful woman in the world,

My wife

Susan Mertz Aman

This book is an excerpt from a comprehensive book on fire

That I am writing and hoping

To have finished soon.

Printed in Great Britain
by Amazon.co.uk, Ltd.,
Marston Gate.